T0197548

Bilingual **Books**

Let's Eat The Colors Of The Rainbow

By Matilde R. Hollander

English • Spanish • Chinese • French • Vietnamese

To order additional copies of this book, contact:
Xlibris
844-714-8691
www.Xlibris.com
Orders@Xlibris.com

ISBN: Softcover   978-1-6641-7853-3
       Hardcover   978-1-6641-7854-0
       EBook   978-1-6641-7852-6

Library of Congress Control Number: 2021911357

Print information available on the last page

Rev. date: 01/22/2022

In loving memory of Professor Povindar
Kumar Mehta

Thank you

Elsa Ayache
French Translator

My-Loc Cao
Vietnamese Translator

Rose Ernst *Illustrator*
lives in Berkeley, CA. where she grew up with her
brothers, sister and loving parents, her passions are
drawings and singing.
Rose recently graduated from High School and is
going on to study
illustration at California State University East Bay.

Utsha Rai
Book cover Illustrator

Joan Thompson,
English Editor,
Registered Dietition Nutritionist

Joanna Larson
Chinese Translator

Maelie Galarza
French Translator

Dedicated to Jonathan, family, teachers, parents and grandparents with gratitud

Reading to your child aloud in your primary language is the best gift you can possibly give. Keep in mind that parents are the first teachers.

A teacher trainer who specializes in early child education with emphasis in bilingual education, she aims to bring awareness to the dire importance of bilingual education in today's increasingly diversifying and globalized world.

Matilde R. Hollander, born in Chile, a Bilingual Certificated Teacher
B.A. The University of Berkeley, CA.
M.B.A from The National Hispanic University, San José CA.

¿Haz visto alguna vez un arco iris formándose en el cielo después de una tormenta?

你见过暴风雨后，挂半边天的彩虹吗？

Có bao giờ em thấy cầu vồng bắc qua nửa bầu trời sau cơn mưa không?

As-tu déjà vu un arc-en-ciel dans le ciel après l'orage ?

Have you ever seen a
rainbow arching half
way across the sky
after a rain storm?

Have you ever seen a rainbow arching half way across the sky after a rain storm?

¿Cuántos colores diferentes puedes ver en el arco iris?

你看见彩虹有几种颜色？

Em thấy bao nhiêu màu trong cầu vồng?

Combien de couleurs différentes vois-tu dans un arc-en-ciel ?

8

Have you ever seen a rainbow arching half way across the sky after a rain storm?

How many different colors do you see in a rainbow?

Las frutas y vegetales, son también de diferentes colores al igual que el arco iris que vemos en el cielo.

水果和蔬菜也有各种颜色，

就像天上的彩虹一样

Rau trái cũng có nhiều màu như vậy.

Giống như cầu vồng em thấy trên trời.

Les fruits et les légumes sont eux aussi de différentes couleurs. Comme l'arc-en-ciel que tu vois dans le ciel.

Have you ever seen a rainbow arching half way across the sky after a rain storm?

Fruits and vegetables come in many different colors too, just like the rainbow you see in the sky.

¿Qué vas a elegir hoy día?

今天你会选择什么吃呢？

Hôm nay em chọn ăn gì nào?

Que veux-tu manger aujourd'hui ?

What will you choose to eat today?

¿Manzana roja?

Manzana roja, pimentán, cereza, tomates, fresas, frambuesa, granadina.

红色的？

苹果、红甜椒、樱桃、西红柿、草莓、树莓、石榴

Thứ gì màu đỏ?

Táo đỏ, ớt chuông đỏ, cherry, cà chua, dâu tây, dâu rừng, lựu

Quelque chose de rouge ?

Pomme, poivron rouge, cerise, tomate, fraise, framboise, grenade ?

What will you choose to eat today?

Something red?

Apple, red pepper, cherry,
tomato, strawberry, raspberry, pomegranate.

¿Algo Amarillo?

Piña, tomate, maiz/elote,
limón, zapallo/calabacita, pimentón amarillo

黄色的？

菠萝、玉米、柠檬、南瓜

Thứ gì màu vàng?

Thơm (dứa), cà chua, bắp, ớt chuông vàng, chanh vàng, bí

Quelque chose de jaune ?

Ananas, tomate, maïs, poivron jaune, citron, courge ?

What will you choose to eat today?

Something yellow?

Pineapple, tomato, corn, lemon, squash, bell pepper.

¿Algo anaranjado?

Calabaza, batata, mandarina, pimiento, bellota, durazno, mango papaya y zanahoria.

橙色的？

南瓜、地瓜、橙子、橘子、西柚、血橙

Thứ gì màu cam?

Bí đỏ, khoai lang, cam, ớt chuông cam, cà chua cam, bí acorn, quýt, bưởi, blood-orange

Quelque chose d'orange ?

Citrouille, patate douce, poivron, orange, tomate, courge, mandarine, pamplemousse, orange sanguine ?

What will you choose to eat today?

Something orange?

Pumpkin, sweet potato, tangerine, pepper, acorn squash, peach, mango, papaya and carrot.

¿Algo verde?

Lechuga, manzana, lima, uvas, hojas verdes, pera, palta/avocado, repollo, bruselas, espinacas.

绿色的？

生菜、青苹果、青柠、绿葡萄、梨、牛油果、包菜、菠菜

Thứ gì màu xanh lục?

Xà lách, táo xanh, chanh xanh, nho xanh, rau xanh collard, lê, trái bơ, bắp cải, bắp cải brussels, rau bó sợi

Quelque chose de vert ?

Laitue, pomme, citron vert, raisin, poire, avocat, chou, chou de Bruxelles, épinard ?

Something green?

Lettuce, apple, lime, grapes, collard greens, pear, avocado, cabbage, brussels sprouts, spinach.

What will you choose to eat today?

¿Algo azul o morado?

Arándano, uvas concord, berenjena, repollo morado, remolacha, nabo, papa morada.

蓝色或紫色的？

蓝莓、茄子、紫甘蓝、黑莓、李子、唐莴苣、甜菜根

Thứ gì màu xanh hay màu tím?

Dâu xanh, nho concord, cà dê, bắp cải tím, dâu đen, mận, cải Thụy Sĩ, củ cải đường, rutabaga, khoai tây tím

Quelque chose de bleu ou de violet ?

Myrtille, raisin sec, aubergine, chou rouge, mûre, prune, betterave, rutabaga ?

Something blue or purple?

Blueberry, concord grapes, eggplant, purple cabbage, blackberry, plum, beets, purple potato.

23

¿Algo blanco o color canela?

Jícama, maíz, coliflor, champiñones, pera marrón, plátano, cebolla, ruibarbo.

褐色或白色的？

（事实上：这是在彩虹里的。只是彩虹是把白色折射成七种颜色。）

Thứ gì màu nâu hay màu trắng?

Củ đậu (hay củ sắn), bắp trắng, bông cải trắng, nấm, lê nâu, chuối, rhubarb

Quelque chose de beige ou de blanc ?

Jicama, maïs, chou-fleur, champignon, poire, banane, rhubarbe.

Something tan or white?

(Fact: this is exactly in the rainbow. But the rainbow splits white light into the 7 colors)

What will you choose to eat today?

Jicama, corn, cauliflower, mushroom, brown pear, banana, onion, rhubarb.

La próxima que veas un arco iris en el cielo, piensa que tu puedes tener en tu plato un arco iris de frutas y vegetales para servirse diariamente.

下次你看见彩虹，记得你每天可以吃彩虹颜色的水果和蔬菜。

Lần tới khi nào thấy cầu vồng trên trời, em hãy nhớ là hàng ngày em có thể ăn rau trái có nhiều màu như cầu vồng nhé.

La prochaine fois que tu vois un arc-en-ciel dans le ciel, rappelle-toi que tu peux avoir un arc-en-ciel avec des fruits et des légumes que tu peux manger tous les jours.

The next time you see a rainbow in the sky, remember that you can have a rainbow of fruits and vegetables every day.

¿Tú sabes como las frutas y los vegetales crecen?

你知道吗？水果和蔬菜如何长得？

Em có biết? ...
Cây ăn trái và rau cải lớn lên như thế nào không?

Sais-tu... comment poussent les fruits et les légumes ?

Do you know how fruits and vegetables grow?

29

El sol provee la energía para que la planta crezca.

阳光提供蔬菜水果生长所需的能量。

Mặt trời cho cây năng lượng để lớn.

Le soleil donne de l'énergie pour que les plantes poussent.

The sun provides energy for the plant to grow.

La lluvia nos provee el agua.

雨水提供水分。

Mưa cho nước.

La pluie fournit l'eau.

Do you know how the rain provides water?

El aire que nos rodea proporciona dióxido de carbono.

我们周围的空气提供二氧化碳。

Không khí quanh ta cho thán khí.

L'air qui nous entoure fournit le dioxyde de carbone.

Do you know the air that surrounds us provides carbon dioxide?

La tierra rica en nutrición proporciona la comida que la planta necesita para crecer.

丰富的土壤提供它们生长所需的养分。

Đất màu mỡ cho cây thức ăn để lớn

La terre fertile offre la nourriture pour faire pousser les plantes qui ont besoin de grandir.

Con estos cuatro ingredientes, la planta tiene todo lo que necesita para crecer y estar saludable.

有了这四种成分，植物才能健康成长。

Bốn chất liệu này cho cây đủ những thứ cần thiết để lớn và khỏe mạnh.

Avec ces quatre ingrédients, les plantes ont tout ce qu'il leur faut pour pousser et être en bonne santé.

With these four ingredients, the plant has all it needs to grow and be healthy.

¿Qué necesitas para crecer
y estar saludable?

你需要什么才能健康成长呢？

Còn em, em cần những gì để lớn và
khỏe mạnh?

De quoi as-tu besoin pour grandir
et être en bonne santé ?

Do you know what you need to grow and be healthy?

What do you need to grow and be healthy?

Necesitas frutas, vegetales,y otros alimentos ,
agua fresca y aire limpio para tener una buena salud
y aún más, un torrente de cuidado y de mucho amor.

你需要水果、蔬菜和其他食物去平衡，如
水、新鲜的空气和无尽的关心与爱护。

Em cần trái cây, rau cải và các thức ăn khác để
giữ cân bằng, cần nước, không khí trong sạch,
và thật nhiều yêu thương và chăm sóc.

Tu as besoin de fruits, de légumes et de
beaucoup d'autres aliments, d'eau, d'air, de plein
d'amour et d'attention.

Do you know what you need?
You need fruits, vegetables and other
foods, water, clean air with showers of
love and care.

43

The Nutrition Rainbow

Tips: *The more naturally colorful your meal is, the more likely it is to have an abundance of cancer-fighting nutrients. Pigments that give fruits and vegetables their bright colors represent a variety of protective compounds. The chart below shows the cancer-fighting and immune-boosting power of different-hued foods.*

Colors	Foods	Colorful Protective Substances and Possible Actions
Red	Tomatoes and tomato products, watermelon, guava	Lycopene: antioxidant; cuts prostate cancer risk
Orange	Carrots, yams, sweet potatoes, mangos, pumpkins	Beta-carotene: supports immune system; powerful antioxidant
Yellow-orange	Oranges, lemons, grapefruits, papayas, peaches	Vitamin C, flavonoids: inhibit tumor cell growth, detoxify harmful substances
Green	Spinach, kale, collards, and other greens	Folate: builds healthy cells and genetic material
Green-white	Broccoli, Brussels sprouts, cabbage, cauliflower	Indoles, lutein: eliminate excess estrogen and carcinogens
White-green	Garlic, onions, chives, asparagus	Allyl sulfides: destroy cancer cells, reduce cell division, support immune systems
Blue	Blueberries, purple grapes, plums	Anthocyanins: destroy free radicals
Red-purple	Grapes, berries, plums	Resveratrol: may suppress estrogen activity
Brown	Whole grains, legumes	Fiber: removes carcinogens

PhysiciansCommittee
for Responsible Medicine   www.PhysiciansCommittee.org • 202-686-2210

17288-NTR/20

Let's eat the colors of the
RAINBOW

Matilde Hollander is a Montessori Bilingual Teacher and Author who decided to stay busy during retirement by specializing in bilingual book readings. She is widely recognized as a bilingual presenter and advocate. Her presentations are fun and often feature music. She provides research and presentations to new teachers in the field of bilingual education. She reads at public libraries and is an avid advocate for early age second language acquisition.

Other multilingual books by the author

My Five Senses edition I

and edition II

Directions

Book number 4

Illustrations: **Rose Ernst**

Design: **Nas Khan**

English: **Joan Thompson**

Chinese Translation: **Joanna Larson**

French Translation: **Maelie Galarza, Elsa Ayache**

Vietnamese Translation: **My-Loc Cao**

Spanish Translation: **Matilde R. Hollander**

Other multilingual books by the author
My Five Senses edition I
and edition II
Directions

The idea of "eating a rainbow" transforms eating fruit and vegetables into a kid-friendly treasure hunt! My boys have always enjoyed the challenge of searching for foods that match each color of the rainbow. It's such a simple, affirmative approach to build good nutrition habits and a positive psychology around eating. -Anna Dorman, mother and health educator

"So much in one small book! The rainbow theme and colorful illustrations encourage interest and discussion about healthy food and keeping ourselves healthy, The wonderful page is the worms and bugs helping the soil Perfect for preschoolers and kindergarten children ". -Nan Smekofsky, retired preschool/kindergarten teacher

Printed in the United States
by Baker & Taylor Publisher Services